REAL Women On The Journey

A Traveler's Guide for Everyday Life

*Stories and insights provided
by the REAL Women Core Team*

Purposed Publishing Company,
Bowie, MD

REAL Women On The Journey:
A Traveler's Guide for Everyday Life

Copyright © 2017 by REAL Women

Purposed Publishing Company
1019 Fallcrest Ct.
Bowie, MD 20721

ISBN-13:   ISBN 978-0-692-98375-1

Cover design by Stephen Fortune at Skycon Media, LLC
Editing and Proofreading by Bathsheba Smithen

Printed in the United States of America

To the woman who desperately seeks to be free
and travel lighter, this book is for you.

Contents

I Am Not the Same

by NEPHATERIA MCBRIDE

I moved a couple of weekends ago from Virginia to Maryland. As I was packing up the contents of my home, I had many moments where a picture, greeting card, or some other memento caused me to pause for a moment to reflect. While reflecting, some of those moments made me burst out in laughter. Some made a huge smile spread across my face and some of those moments made my eyes fill with tears. All in all, as I sat and reflected... I realized that the broken, wounded, lost woman who walked into that apartment four years ago was not the same woman that was preparing to leave the apartment.

The truth is that I had no clue about who I was when I moved into that apartment in Alexandria, VA in September 2013. I had been divorced for two years. I was fresh out of a rebound relationship that had almost killed me. My oldest daughter and grandbaby were living in PA, and I had just dropped my youngest daughter off at college in Miami. I was a new empty nester and was wandering through life simply trying to survive. But that woman is not the woman who emerged from the apartment two weeks ago. I have grown. I have changed. I am FREE and am no longer a slave to the bondage that held me in chains when I walked into that apartment. I am whole! I am light! I am powerful! I am authentically ME! I am a Warrior Princess!! And my metamorphosis happened in the REAL Women Sister Circle.

I am a firm believer that we grow best in circles. I have experienced growth sitting in the pews of the church, but I increased exponentially in the REAL Women Sister Circle.

Listen!!

My life has been radically changed because of my participation in the REAL Women Sister Circles. The women in this circle have loved me unconditionally and have provided a safe place where I can just be. They have lovingly challenged me to do the soul work necessary to walk in freedom and be the best me that I can be. They have wiped my tears. They held my hand and supported me when I lost family members. They didn't pass judgment on me when I kept returning to an emotionally abusive relationship but challenged me to love and value myself. They showed up ready to wreck shop when I was sexually assaulted earlier this year. They have shared in my joys. They have encouraged me. I could go on and on about how this circle has blessed my life!! The bottom line is that they have helped shape me into the woman that I am today. I walked into that apartment a broken, wounded soul but emerged a powerful, free Warrior Princess. And I owe that to the REAL Women Sister Circle.

Questions for Reflection

1. What radical changes have you seen in your life over the past few years?

2. What support systems do you have or need in place to bring about the future change you want to see?

_____

_____

_____

_____

_____

_____

_____

_____

_____

_____

_____

_____

_____

_____

_____

_____

_____

_____

A Beautiful Mess

by SHAVON CARTER

Recently I got an old tattoo recolored. When reading up on how to care for it (because I forgot when I got it the first time), it said to wash it with antibacterial soap and keep it moisturized. The article said once it starts to peel, don't pick at any scabbing, just let it fall off over time or during the gentle cleaning process. It warned that picking at the scar can ruin the tattoo or cause light spots that will have to be touched up.

Although I read the warning, I noticed how uncomfortable I felt seeing my tattoo peeling and not being able to fix it and make it look pretty. When I looked down at my arm, I didn't want to see the mess; I wanted to see the beautiful finished product. It would be nice if I could cover it up until it was healed, but the instructions also said to keep it uncovered so that it can breathe. Recently, I realized I not only felt this way about my tattoo; but that's also how I see myself. I'm currently going through a healing process, and a lot about me is surfacing. Like the tattoo, I want to hurry and fix what I see "wrong" with me so I can look and feel better. Today, as I was venting to my sister-friends, one of them asked me, "What is your truth?" I typed the scary things that I didn't want to admit to myself or anybody else. Afterwards, I felt numb and wanted to escape from myself.

That was my pattern. I face the truth, and then I want to distract myself to avoid feeling what it's like to sit with the truth. But at that moment, I wanted to try something different. I asked myself, "What does wholeness look like in this space?" My answer to myself was, "It looks like a beautiful mess." Wholeness looked like admitting my truths, owning my flaws, and standing up in it. Wholeness was seeing my faults AND seeing myself as the masterpiece God created. I didn't need to be covered up. I needed to see myself exposed. Instead of beating myself up as I would typically do, I sat with myself and just affirmed me. I let ME know that it was okay to be where I was. The moment was perfect and necessary. It provided an opportunity for me to extend love and acceptance to myself, just like I do with others. Just like God does with me. It didn't serve me to judge myself for how I got into this mess; that didn't matter. What matters is that I'm healing by learning how to embrace me in the tough times and see these moments as precious. What matters is that I'm practicing connecting with myself on a deeper level. A level I had never gone to before… The level of creating true intimacy, in a mess. As a result, I could see myself standing up tall in my mess. It was beautiful!

We all have flaws, but how often are we able to be with those flaws and gently love ourselves through it all? If you're like me and have a habit of beating yourself up when you see your imperfections, I invite you to try a different approach. Love on you the way you would love on a little child who came to you with their flaws. You're worthy of giving yourself that kind of love. I know you want to "pick at your scabs" through judgment and rush through the process so you can "look" better, but doing so may result in going through it all over again. So imagine what it would feel like to look at your WHOLE self in the mirror and accept where you are. Envision what it feels like to love YOU through it. Visualize the strength that would develop. Feel the peace and connection you would experience. Find the beauty in embracing all of YOU, including the mess. It's beautiful!

Questions for Reflection

1. What personal flaws do you have a hard time accepting?

2. What would it take for you to accept your flaws and see yourself as whole?

_____

_____

_____

_____

_____

_____

_____

_____

_____

_____

_____

_____

_____

_____

_____

_____

What Are You Wearing?

by KEAH MASON

This summer, I began dating a nice guy who I started to like very quickly. Perhaps I was rushing to finally have the boyfriend I've always wanted. Although I could tell the attraction and interest were mutual, I felt like something was missing, and it was…his effort. Maybe he just wasn't ready to give his full attention, and although I sensed there was something restricting him, I kept pushing. I had his initial interest, and I was determined to keep it. So I pressed and pushed. I called, I texted…a lot, a whole lot. Things were fine when I got the response and feedback I wanted, but when I didn't get what I was reaching for, I lost it. I lost my mind, my peace, and my faith.

I've always had insecurities, but I was convinced that I had improved through the self-care practices I'd been implementing for the past year. But what I didn't know was that my insecurities were still there, and they were rooted in fear. Because I've always been single and hurt too many times to count, I was scared. I still believed in true love, and I still wanted it, but I didn't know that my behavior was toxic and sabotaging.

I claimed to care about the guy I was dating, and that I was just simply worried about him, but in reality, I was just co-dependent. Yep, I needed him to give me constant and consistent affirmation to reassure me that WE were okay. Every day, I needed to know that he was still interested and he still wanted me.

If he didn't call or text me right back, or plan for us to spend time together, how was I supposed to know for sure that he was still interested? I needed the verification, and I felt lost without it. And instead of just moving on and letting it go, I pushed harder. I needed him to tell me the truth. I couldn't trust in what I observed. I needed to hear it from him, and when he didn't provide that every single day, I panicked.

My panic made me anxious, and my anxiety caused me to behave in a toxic manner. So I wasn't reaching out just because I cared. I was reaching out because I was dependent on him to fill the voids I had in my life. When I finally stooped to the lowest level of being "pressed," I finally saw myself. At last, I was able to see that I was acting scary, needy, clingy, possessive, desperate, insecure, and co-dependent. All of those elements are rooted in fear because I was afraid that he was going to leave me as everyone else had. But, I'm not even attracted to those qualities.

So now that I could finally acknowledge those traits in myself, I made a decision. I decided I wasn't going to hate that girl. I understood her, and I felt compassion for her. Of course, she's scared. Of course, she needs reassurance because she's been left multiple times by men who didn't bother to say goodbye or provide any explanation. Of course, she panics because she just wants someone to be responsive and attentive. She's human! So, not pointing fingers or throwing shade at her, but instead, I chose to love her. I looked her right in the eyes and told her that she's beautiful and that she is in fact loved, right now. For the first time in 35 years, I held her gaze and told her that I loved her.

I didn't put her down, and I didn't want her to feel ashamed. I just told her that this is a growth opportunity to live and embrace an abundant life that is no longer bound by fear. Emphasizing that nothing was wrong with her, I just told her it's time to change her clothes. I reminded her of a quote by Amanda Patterson that says, "The way you communicate reveals everything about you. Words are the clothes your thoughts wear". So, I said, let's put on a new outfit, one that reveals wholeness and trust in God.

She just needed a new look because she wasn't going to keep dressing in shame, fear, rejection, loneliness, brokenness, co-dependence, and hurt. Yes, she felt that way sometimes but why keep putting that on every single day? I told her, God will clothe you in the essence of His character. You don't have to keep walking around in the same old clothes just because you've always had them.

As I expressed my adoration for her, I assured her that she is enough. With understanding, I told her it's okay for her to trust God to increase her faith in spite of her fears. So while it's completely natural to be upset, frustrated, and confused by someone else's actions, it's imperative that you understand that God is higher than those feelings. He is the source of your strength, and you can only find this ideal love you're looking for, in Him. No other person will ever be able to love unconditionally and perfectly.

So yes, you're going to have feelings, and that's okay. But while you have feelings and wants, just know that you can trust for it to be provided. God is already providing it. When it doesn't come in the way you want it to, just know that God has you and you are always okay. That's what I told her, and guess what? With a heart that still hurts sometimes, she decided to walk as if she is loved because she is.

Questions for Reflection

1. Regardless of someone else's actions, and in spite of how you feel, what "clothes" are you going to put on today?

2. In what ways are you already being loved?

3. The traits that you possess are like gems. Identify your traits and how you plan to value and appreciate them.

_____

_____

_____

_____

_____

_____

_____

_____

_____

_____

_____

_____

_____

_____

Just Show Up

by KEAH MASON

It was just hours before I needed to get on the road to drive to the REAL Women launch in Hampton Roads. I wasn't ready to make the trip because I had just made a horrible mistake. Consumed with guilt and shame, I wasn't ready to enter a room filled with women for a sister circle where I'd have to pretend to be okay. But, I wanted to be supportive, so reluctantly, with a heavy heart, I packed my car and headed to Virginia.

As I drove, I began to pray and ask God for His forgiveness. I admitted my mistakes and explained that I had no intention of repeating my past behavior. As I prayed, God began to exchange my shame for hope. He showed me that I would have an opportunity to do better and that I still had the chance to stand and walk in my truth. This excited me and I began to feel a little better. God had taken the burden off of my shoulder and cleansed me with forgiveness and hope for a brighter future, not haunted by my past mistakes.

I had been so afraid to make the trip to Hampton Roads because of my burdened heart, but God gave me many beautiful surprises that weekend. In no hurry to return to Maryland, I needed to stay in the Hampton Roads area on Saturday evening before heading to Williamsburg the next day. When my initial plans didn't work out, my REAL Women sister, Ms. Sylvia welcomed me into her beautiful home. With warmth, hospitality, sincerity, and a delicious bowl of oatmeal for breakfast, Ms. Sylvia showed me the love of Jesus. I was so amazed that someone would invite me into their home and take such good care of me. As we shared conversation over breakfast, Ms. Sylvia said that when people come to her home, she wants them to feel Jesus. I certainly did.

The entire weekend was filled with laughter, fun in the pool, great food, awesome company, and a day spent at my favorite water park! I was left feeling so grateful for God's forgiveness. He showered His unconditional love on me all weekend, and I felt so full. It was such a loving, gentle reminder that God loves us no matter what and when He demonstrates His perfect love through others, we are reassured that we'll be okay.

No matter how you feel, just show up anyway. When you choose to show up, God will always meet you there.

Questions for Reflection

1. What burdens are you carrying in your heart today, that keep you from showing up in life?

2. What would it look like to release those burdens and live lighter? Are you willing to do that today?

_____

_____

_____

_____

_____

_____

_____

_____

_____

_____

_____

_____

_____

_____

_____

_____

Here

by BATHSHEBA SMITHEN

Anger was comfortable, so I wore it as a garment to keep others from noticing my pain. I felt ashamed and disgraced. The torment boring into my soul made me age without actually growing older. Here was where I desperately wanted to be, but my need to be liberated was not as great as my need to feel protected, so the walls of my psychological fortress remained intact.

It's hard to let yourself embody each moment as it occurs. You either lean on the past's burdens or fall forward, pressing your hopes against an intangible future. I was neither here nor over there. I was caught in a parallel universe, rehearsing again and again what I could have done to secure my innocence while my body stood in the present, trying to focus my mind on my current situation.

She was calling me, beckoning me to be here. But being here felt too frightening. It would force me to lay aside every brick, every layer of wall that enclosed and shielded me from those who might hurt me. I wanted to be free, but not at the expense of being filled with enormous pain. Removing the layers would force me to acknowledge the stains mounted like memorials on my heart. I didn't want to write a eulogy for my pain; I wanted to piss on the grave of my dysfunction and summon the dark forces that had killed my joy, to murder the happiness of anyone connected to the traumas I had endured. In other words, I wanted to forget the past, but I didn't want the past to forget that I owed it vengeance, and revenge is impossible without holding onto the memories that locked you up in the first place.

When does one finally heal? Depression mounts like fear personified; it builds itself an empire and aspires to reach the heavens and become your god. My Babel started when I drew closer to the things that would hide self. It made me forget who I saw in the mirror. It made me paint her with rags and riches to cover my true decisions to be a witness to my own death.

The REAL Women Intensive by the Water was monumental for me. The healing process that began is beyond words. It's so far out of the reach of what I can convey because what I experienced cannot be written in a summary, a short story, a poem, or song. It is etched on the walls of my soul; reverberating in the beat of my heart. You see, the sessions on spirituality, sexual healing, big rocks, boundaries, our stories, and self-worth, unlocked places within that allowed the little girl within to merge with the present; to find her way through the barriers of my stubbornness.

I'm now in the process of moving out of the space that had me stuck between here and there. It was during the intensive and only then that I came to realize the ten years of my childhood that had been stored away in a vault by me. While I have been in therapy, my sessions have become more profound and freeing. There is something about keys that make their way into deadbolt locks: they find a way to enter into a place the homeowner has worked hard to keep sealed off. Let's just say; the intensive started the release of me from my own cage; one I decorated and designed. I truly am becoming cage free from the traumas that I hadn't cared to remember.

Maybe that's you too.

I believe that while we all are afraid of our past, we strongly desire to make the terror disappear. The only way to ease the pain of terror is, we must step out of the intermediate space between here and there. Until then, our here will be in the past, and our present will remain obsolete.

I challenge you to step out; to face your fears head-on to become the REAL and authentic you.

Questions for Reflection

1. What fears have you not allowed yourself to face?

2. What would it look like to face those fears head-on to become the REAL and authentic you?

_____

_____

_____

_____

_____

_____

_____

_____

_____

_____

_____

_____

_____

_____

_____

_____

_____

Recovering the Lost Files

by ASHLEY GILBERT

Will the real Ashley Gilbert please stand up?!

I am Felix Gilbert's wife, the mother of three wonderful children, a life coach, friend and blah blah blah. These are all titles. Everything I listed has to do with who I am to someone else, not who I am to myself. I mean, don't get me wrong, I am proud to be a wife and mother. But somewhere along the last ten years, I have gotten lost under these titles, loads of laundry and wifely duties.

At some point, I realized I didn't know who I wanted to be anymore. So a few years ago I vowed to seek out and find every lost file and to define my true authentic self. I took time to affirm my body, mind, and spirit so that I could emerge full of self-love. This year I have committed to seeing every facet of me, (the good, bad and ugly) extending grace and taking my power back.

I am tired of letting others and their expectations of me be the defining measure of my greatness. Most of my 20's were spent being something to and for others. Now in my 30's I am going to be me. Only God can truly define who and what that means to be Ashley Alexandria Gilbert.

I pledge first to acknowledge every barrier, and then do the work to tear them down so I can be free to walk in the complete freedom of being myself. I release every negative judgment towards myself. I stand knowing that every broken piece of me doesn't need to be thrown away, but mended and healed. I recognize that the broken places in me allow God's light to shine through.

Questions for Reflection

1. What do you need to do to either define or redefine the REAL you? Are there barriers or strongholds that are preventing you from clearly exemplifying all that you are? Do you need to go through a process of recovering your lost files?

2. Who is the REAL you?

3. Write your own pledge. What affirmation will help remind you of who you are?

Can you clearly answer these questions? If not, do the work and BE you!

I Am Not Alone

by KEAH MASON

On this journey to wholeness and freedom, I feel a mixture of emotions. It's uncomfortable, scary, overwhelming, beautiful, humbling, and exciting. So yeah, it's a wide range of feelings. Being baggage free, cage free, and shame-free means that I have to deal with one of my biggest issues…being alone.

I'm ashamed of being alone, and my job makes it even harder for me. I'm an elementary school teacher. Teaching is the joy of my life, but it can also seem very abusive. It's a tough job, and there are days when I just don't feel appreciated or respected. I walk out of the building with my head down and sometimes I just desire for someone to tell me it's going to be okay. I just need a hug. I want to sit down to a nice meal at my dinner table and talk to someone about my day so that they can offer love and encouragement, but guess what? It's just me.

Who is going to pour into me after a challenging day? I think about this often, and it's frustrating, but just when I need to be picked up and loved on…God provides. I am single, but I'm not forgotten, and I'm often in need of that reminder. God knows how delicate, fragile, and sensitive I am and I've been amazed at how He's taken care of me in the sweetest ways.

Today was one of those tough days at work, but one of my REAL Women sister-friends reached out to me and told me that she had packed up some food for me to take home. I love to eat, and I love even more that I didn't have to cook, but she offered me something more than food. She extended God's love to me at just the right time. Through her act of kindness and sharing, God reminded me that He loves me and that He's here for me. I got the hug I needed this evening all because I'm connected to the most-high God who is ALWAYS attentive to my needs. That connection with Him has connected me with others who are a reflection of Him. And because of that, guess what? I'm not alone! You're not alone! We have each other to lean on. We do not have to walk this road by ourselves…ever!

On this journey to wholeness and freedom, God keeps reminding me that I am not alone. He sees me, He hears me, and He has me on His mind.

Questions for Reflection

1. Has there ever been a time where you were afraid to spend time with yourself? If so, why?

2. In what ways have you been shown that you are not alone on your journey?

3. How can you help show others than they are not alone?

_____

_____

_____

_____

_____

_____

_____

_____

_____

_____

_____

_____

_____

_____

_____

Ask for What You Need

by KEAH MASON

As an adult, I realized that I was truly saddened by my lack of gifts and talents. I couldn't sing, dance, sew, bake, draw, or anything. No athletic or artistic abilities at all and that stressed me out. I shared this with two friends, and they said they believed that I had a talent for being thoughtful and caring for others. Is that really even a gift?

I love buying cards and gifts for others. I'm that person that remembers special occasions, and in every friend circle I'm a part of, I'm the one who encourages the get-togethers. I'm the planner, and the one who sends cards randomly and I absolutely love it. I'm the giver in that way, but what happens when I need to be on the receiving end?

For the last three birthdays, I planned my own birthday celebrations because I didn't want to be disappointed when no one else mentioned anything. I took control of the situation because I just knew that no one would plan anything because typically, that's MY role. But, when I finished my Master's program for graduate school, I really, really, really wanted to celebrate and I didn't want to be the one to initiate it.

Although I had decided not to participate in the commencement ceremony, I was hoping that someone would send a card or plan a party or something. I thought that someone in my family or one of my close friends would plan something, or send me a graduation gift (let me just keep it real). That didn't happen, and as I was busy making baskets and gift packages for other people, which I LOVE to do, I was still hurt because I just knew…no one was going to do that for me, and I wanted them to.

I literally cried out to God and thanked Him for the way I'm wired…to be thoughtful and caring towards others. That's pretty effortless for me, and just maybe, that is my gift and talent. But again, what happens when I need to be the recipient? I told God how I felt and I was honest. It just hurts to always be the one to do for others, but when you give in that way, ironically, it's kinda rare that you receive in the same way.

But once again, God beautifully surprised me. At the REAL Women Mastering the Balancing Act Boot Camp during the same week I had cried out to God about no one celebrating my graduation, Trenace called me up to the front and publically celebrated me. It was such a special moment, and it's one that I'll never forget.

As I sit here this evening, my heart is so full. Once again, God heard me and let me know that I'm not forgotten. And how awesome is it to be a part of a sister community where we celebrate each other so lovingly and unselfishly? When people hugged me with tears in their eyes and said "Congratulations," I could literally feel that they we rejoicing with me. As someone who's learning more and more every day about self-care and self-acceptance, that's huge for me.

We all have gifts and talents, and it's okay for us to tell others what we need. We don't have to hide behind the mask of pretending to be okay when our needs or wants aren't met. And above all else, God always knows what we need, and He always provides in the most surprising and profound ways.

Questions for Reflection

1. In what ways do you see your needs being provided for?

2. What do you need to reach out and ask for today?

Life Is No Fairytale

by DR. TRENACE RICHARDSON

So I have a thing for frogs...

It's weird to some and charming to a few, but it's real. I really love frogs. When most people run, not walk, the other way when they see frogs hop into their driveway or onto a park playground, I'm usually trying to pick it up to see if I can get it to calm down in my palm. I even have a picture of me at a pier one day, looking like I'm about to kiss a frog.

I know. Why admit this, right?

Well, I'm willing to talk about it here because I recognize that a small portion of this affection I have with frogs has to do with the whole prince turning into a frog thing. You know...this fairytale storyline...

There are other reasons too. I love loving the underdog, the one that no one likes or counts on to win. I also love the metamorphosis a frog undergoes as it develops and matures. A frog's look and life at its beginning are very different from its ending. And my sister girlfriend, Ashley Gilbert, gave me a card some time ago that provided me with several more reasons to love frogs.

But, as quiet as it's kept, I've always loved the idea of a fantasy romance or a fairytale kind of life. You know, the kind of Cinderella story that takes a poor, ordinary girl and turns her into a wealthy princess who is the envy of all around her.

Whenever I've found myself longing for more money, influence, success, or romance...

I've had to remind myself that fantasies don't exist and fairytales aren't real. I've had to remember that NO ONE is living a fantasy life and if they look like they are, I don't know enough of their story. And if they say they are, they are lying. They have either had it rough, have it rough now, or will have it rough in the future.

I know I sound like a killjoy, but if I don't say things aloud to myself sometimes, I will disillusion myself into longing for someone else's life or some other version of my own life. Different than the one I am currently blessed enough to live out. I'm wondering if you have been there or if you are there now...

Questions for Reflection

1. What fairy tale are you holding onto that needs to be released?

2. How have fantasies negatively impacted your happiness?

3. What realities can you appreciate about your life right now?

_____

_____

_____

_____

_____

_____

_____

_____

_____

_____

_____

_____

_____

_____

Hiding Behind a "Fit" Body

by ASHLEY GILBERT

Somewhere along the way, I lost my discipline, my drive and motivation to always eat healthily and be healthy. In high school and college, I was very athletic. I ran track, played volleyball and danced. Being fit and healthy was never an issue, or so I thought. See, it wasn't that I was necessarily healthy; I just had a fit body. I didn't eat the way that I should; I ate like a typical high school or college student. I was able to hide behind the fact that I was "a good weight for my height." Well before my last three semesters of college, I got married, and two months before my internship was to start I had my first child (can you say honeymoon baby?). But of course like many people do during their first pregnancy and marriage, you gain weight. My problem was that I was on bed rest from 5 months pregnant until the end because of major complications that almost caused me to miscarry.

So there I was a newlywed, pregnant on bedrest, and stuck at home. Enclosed behind four walls; an emotional WRECK!!!! So what did I do??? I ate. I began to not care. The first year of my marriage was a very challenging one on many levels, yet it taught me my real character. Behind my fit body was a person with a distorted view of what healthy meant. I felt that as long as I looked good, I was ok. But the truth is a healthy lifestyle and mindset have nothing really to do with what you look like and more to do with a lifestyle pattern. I wasn't healthy because deep down even though I looked acceptable to the rest of the world; I wasn't accepting myself. So after my pregnancy and through the tough first year of marriage when I no longer could hide behind a "fit" body, I fell apart. The way I coped was having an attitude of not caring. Sinking into a pit of "this is how it's going to be." I began a vicious cycle of comparing myself to other women and hating myself even more for it. It was through a series of events and times in my life the past few years where God has slowly but surely been taking me through a process of first loving myself, eating healthier, and becoming fit and active. One of those events was participating in a marathon relay where I completed 6 miles in 1 hour, finishing off the 26 miles for my team! One of these days I will write about my lessons from that! By no means am I where I want to be but I know I'm not where I was in regards to my unhealthy mentality.

I think we should all stop focusing so much on the outside and place our attention on what's most important...our inner being. Our heart and character. That is what God cares about the most. Then and only then do I believe we will be ready to set up healthy weight loss goals and plans that fit US. Find what works for you. Deal with the inside motive for why you want to lose weight. Love the "you" of now so that when you do lose the weight, you will love that self FULLY! Embrace you! Love you and God will lead you to a HEALTHIER YOU! We must first DEPROGRAM all of our NEGATIVE HABITS!!!

Questions for Reflection

1. What negative views about your body and health, are you carrying?

2. What does a healthy life look like for YOU?

3. Many of us have an ideal weight or shape we'd like to be in, but what about your mind? What practices can you put in place to keep your mind in shape?

_____

_____

_____

_____

_____

_____

_____

_____

_____

_____

Fall Colors

by ASHLEY GILBERT

My neighborhood is surrounded by trees and secret paths full of leaves of various sizes. During my walks, I have enjoyed looking at all the different colors and sizes of the leaves. I love walking along paths and hearing the crunch underneath my feet from piles and piles of leaves fallen on the ground. Today, as I was walking to the library with the kids, I had a revelation of how God's process with the fall season is the same in our lives.

Each fall season the leaves begin to change into beautiful colors and then fall off where they will wither and die. From there the trees are in a dormant state until the spring when they will bring forth new green leaves. In our lives, we enter seasons where God takes us through different changes and extremes to prepare us for newness. In this process, sometimes pieces of our character and life wither and die so that something new can spring forth.

Sometimes we would love to remain in the place where we have the beautiful colors, but that isn't where the true blessing and newness lies. We can't abort a season of being dormant due to our impatience. Be sure of this, Spring will come, and in that season something new will "spring" forth.

"For I am about to do something new. See, I have already begun! Do you not see it? I will make a pathway through the wilderness. I will create rivers in the dry wasteland." Isaiah 43:19

As you walk the paths of your life, enjoying your current season, remember God will not leave you in this place. He desires to bring you to something new. He has more for you. The old will become new. Be patient. Be aware of what God is doing.

Questions for Reflection

1. What new things do you notice in this current season of your life?

2. How can you enjoy this current season of your life?

_____

_____

_____

_____

_____

_____

_____

_____

_____

_____

_____

_____

_____

_____

_____

_____

_____

Broken Glass

by ASHLEY GILBERT

This week, several glass items have been shattered all over my kitchen floor. First a measuring cup and then a light fixture. Glass on the floor is a nightmare to clean up. It's as if we never find all of the pieces. And just when you think you have, someone steps on the tiniest shard.

As I vacuumed to clear up the glimmering broken pieces, it hit me. I will never be able to put this light fixture back together or get the measuring cup back, but God in his loving power and kindness intricately has put me back together bit by bit. Piece by piece.

I am reminded, and I want to emphasize to anyone reading, that no matter how broken we are and no matter how tiny the pieces, Christ will find them and put us back together. We will be made new! And the cracks that come after you glue broken glass together allow His light to shine through!

I am thankful for my brokenness because it positioned me to be healed and put back together by my Heavenly Father!

Questions for Reflection

1. Do you feel broken? If so, are you grateful for your broken pieces? Why or why not?

2. How has your brokenness positioned you for healing?

3. If you have fully embraced all of your broken pieces, what is the greatest piece of advice in the process to wholeness that you can provide yourself, should you encounter another storm?

_____

_____

_____

_____

_____

_____

_____

_____

_____

_____

_____

_____

_____

Friendship

by KEAH MASON

I've always had a lot of good girlfriends. From elementary school to college years, church, small group, coworkers, and so on, I've been blessed with friendships. But as I've gotten older, close bonds have become more occasional. I may get a text message now and then, or a comment on Facebook, but gone are the days of talking on the phone for hours. No more hanging out all the time. I no longer have anyone that I speak with on a daily basis, and I must admit, I miss that.

I often realize how much I miss my friends, and sometimes I reach out and take the initiative, but other times, I just stay to myself and remain at the surface where those friendships usually exist. I always know my friends are there for me if I need anything, but it just seems like maybe we're too old or too busy for the day to day conversations.

I went to a friend's wedding yesterday, and while I rejoiced in her happiness, my thoughts wandered to my own circumstances. I thought…Who would be my maid of honor? Who would plan my bridal shower? When I have a baby, who would be the godmother? Who's gonna celebrate my birthday with me? Who's gonna go shopping with me? Who's gonna go on vacation with me?

It's a struggle to admit that because those thoughts seem so selfish, but they are so real. While I appreciate the various friends I have, I miss having a best friend. I miss having someone I can talk with often. I miss the close connection with someone who knows everything about me, and I about them.

While life has changed, my need for connectedness hasn't. I had prayed about it several times this week, and just yesterday, when I returned from my friend's wedding, I was beautifully surprised. I checked my mailbox, and to my amazement, one of my friends had mailed me a random card, just because. The message inside was heartfelt, and it included some money. In short, she said she just wanted to send some love to me, and she wanted me to use the gift to treat myself to something special that makes me smile.

Wow! At that moment, I was reminded that God hears me. My concerns are so valid to Him, and He makes it a priority to show me that He cares. God created us for connections and intimacy. We just have to trust that we're provided with what we need. Our longing for friendships is no surprise to God. Whatever you need today, is no surprise to God.

Questions for Reflection

1. What is the current state of your friendships?

2. What can you do to cultivate current friendships and/or build new ones?

_____

_____

_____

_____

_____

_____

_____

_____

_____

_____

_____

_____

_____

_____

_____

"I haven't been chosen... Is something wrong with me?"

by SHAVON CARTER

Is something wrong with me? I've asked myself that on many occasions and what comes up is a tarnished view of myself as I run down a list of my "wrongs." That list says...

I'm divorced. I've had two abortions. I have a sexual past. I'm skinny. I'm dark-skinned. I wear glasses. My hair is kinky, not straight. The list goes on. As I type this out, I can see that those thoughts are absolutely FALSE because I'm an amazing and beautiful black woman. However, when I'm in those cynical moments, I let my emotions feed off the lies. So what's the "Is something wrong with me?" question really all about? It's rooted in how I see myself. Let me explain.

If I'm a single woman who is asking "is something wrong with me?" simply because someone hasn't decided to be in a romantic relationship with me, I'm pointing to a belief about myself that may have been lying dormant all along. If I were in a relationship, it might show up in another form, like "Am I pretty enough for him to stay?" or "What if he finds someone better than me?" So in the end, it's not really about being "chosen" by a man. It's about what I believe about me. Make sense? So if I'm a single woman who subconsciously doesn't believe that I'm enough in some way, then I will subconsciously look for others to provide what I don't believe about myself. As a result, I begin to crave validation and attention from men to make me feel like I'm worthy and valuable because I don't really believe it for myself.

Many of us single women get trapped in this way of thinking and don't realize it. So how do we break this cycle? Well, it starts with being aware of where we are. It's time for us to know that it's okay not to have it all together. Let's be real and acknowledge that we have insecurities, need to be validated, need to be paid attention to, etc. It's perfectly okay to have emotional needs. The question is, how do we get our emotional needs met healthily? When I say healthy, I mean a balance between offering what we need to ourselves and getting it from others. So basically, I'm not solely relying on someone else to give me what I need. I'm starting with giving it to myself first.

So what are some ways to break up the "Is something wrong with me?" belief? Here are a few suggestions that have been helpful for me:

- Create a list of the amazing things about you, beginning with "I am…"
- Look at yourself in the mirror and speak affirming things
- Pray and read scriptures in the Bible that affirm who you are

- Participate in activities where you get to serve others and use your gifts and talents

- Permit yourself to have sad moments and cry

- Process your emotions with a therapist

- Vent and seek encouragement from close friends and family

- Hire a life coach to help you see yourself as the awesome person you are

This list is just a start, and I'm sure you can add more. Being single doesn't mean you're going to like it every single day. Allow yourself to have your moments, get the support you need, then choose to continue enjoying your life where you are. Most of all, please embrace that there's nothing wrong with you!

Questions for Reflection

1. How do you feel about your current relationship status?

2. If you are discontent and have negative feelings about your status, in what ways can you start to break up those thoughts?

3. How are those feelings connected to your childhood?

_____

_____

_____

_____

_____

_____

_____

_____

_____

_____

_____

_____

_____

_____

_____

Enough Is Enough

by SHAVON CARTER

I just needed to scream. Everything that I'd been holding onto. Every word that I had never uttered. Every unnamed emotion that I felt needed to be released in a scream. As I sat in the company of my sisters in the recovery group, I let it out. I screamed at the top of my lungs like I was fighting for my life. I screamed for the little girl whose father wasn't present. I screamed for the woman who has been looking for love outside of herself. I screamed for the woman who had had enough of the same unhealthy cycle. I screamed for the woman who didn't want to keep it all together anymore. I let it all out, and suddenly everything stood still. The anxiety and anguish were replaced with calm. I felt God's invisible, yet loving arms around me. Letting go was what I needed to do.

Sis, what are you holding onto today? What burdens are you carrying that weigh you down? Aren't you tired of trying to do it all by yourself? Aren't you tired of journeying alone? That baggage wasn't meant for you to keep carrying like an accessory. That pain you experienced was for purpose, not cargo to drag around. I know you've probably been carrying it for so long that it's become a part of you. It would probably be uncomfortable to go without it, but… .what if?

What if you could travel a little lighter? What if you could let go of what keeps you feeling stuck? What if your clipped wings were reattached so you could fly? Imagine what it would feel like to be FREE…

That freedom can start with a simple release. Kick, scream, cry…do whatever you have to do to let it out. There's healing in the release. There's peace in the letting go. Don't worry about what you'll look like or what people will think if they heard or saw you. Just permit yourself to let go and trust God to meet you right there. The next steps to take will come, but in this moment I admonish you to just let go. You'll be so glad you did.

Questions for Reflection

1. What do you need to release today?

2. In what ways will you let go so you can travel lighter?

_____

_____

_____

_____

_____

_____

_____

_____

_____

_____

_____

_____

_____

_____

Human BEINGS by Design

by ASHLEY GILBERT

If you are anything like me, at the start of a new year I list out all of my goals and dreams that I want to have accomplished by year's end. I buy planners, journals, and all the works to ensure I will stay organized and productive throughout the year. I am pretty skilled at list-making. I give myself, maybe three goals in specific categories like Physical Health, Finances, Relationships, and Business. After that, I have to break down each goal into action steps. This process gives me a clear guide and charted course for the next 6–12 months.

Now, this is all well and good, but year after year there seems to be one critical question I rarely ask myself during these yearly planning sessions. Who do I want to BE?

I first heard the question, "Who do I want to BE?" asked of me a few years ago at a REAL Women session. Before then, I had only heard this as a child. Most people ask us that question when we are children, and our answer always consisted of what profession we wanted to enter as adults. I always said, doctor or lawyer, because I knew that's what my family hoped. So you can imagine that a question of this nature caused me to have to do some soul-searching.

This question indeed stretches us to think outside of our usual list and goal-driven selves. I have to dig deeper to know what resonates with my spirit. Once we can answer this question, our DOING changes. Everything we do must then reflect what the BE is at our core. We begin to live and breathe out of our BEING intentionally. I mean we aren't called human BE-INGS for no reason. We were designed to fill our days with meaningful moments. Each day should be intentional and from the soul.

To BE authentic and live abundant, fulfilling lives, each year we have to ask the question who do I want to BE? Then and only then should we fill our planners with realistic goals that align with our BEING.

Trenace once challenged us on the "REAL Women Community ALL Call" to find our one word for the year. I immediately knew mine would be PEACE. Even as I type it out, I feel something shift inside my spirit. This year, if it doesn't align with peace, it has to GO! Trenace also urged us to recognize that who we need to be is already within us; We just need to walk it out.

However, if I am honest, the notion that peace is already within me is hard to believe. I mean, it feels most days I am reaching out externally to find peace everywhere else but inside of me! But what just hit me as I am writing, is the issue may be that all I am DOING doesn't align with PEACE. For peace to be drawn out from my core, I only have to DO things that bring peace and align with my core.

As a full-time mother, wife, and entrepreneur many times I get put on the back burner. This year I know in order to BE at peace I have to be intentional about my self-care. I have strategically planned out monthly outings and activities specifically for me to breathe in peace and release stress. I am excited about the fruit in my life that will grow as a result of focusing on me!

I urge you to ask yourself the question, "Who do I want to BE?" and make every effort to walk out of that authenticity in every moment and every breath God gives you.

Questions for Reflection

1. Who do you want to BE this year?

2. What plans can you put in place that focuses on your BEING?

_____

_____

_____

_____

_____

_____

_____

_____

_____

_____

_____

_____

_____

_____

_____

Is My Light Too Bright for You?

by DR. TRENACE RICHARDSON

Have you ever feared good things happening for you because you didn't really believe you deserved them? I have. It is what I am dealing with right now, in fact. I know that, if I allow it, this will be the most incredible year of my life: for me, my family, my ministry, and my business. And I am certain that the only obstacle in my way is me. But what gives me the right to get out of my own way?

When I look at my adult life, I have done some incredible and amazing things. I have used my gifts and resources to help many. I have nurtured an incredible family and cultivated priceless friendships. I have envisioned and, with God's help, brought to fruition several ministries and a new business. There are so many reasons why I should get out of my own way to allow God to take me further. I know this in my head, but my heart feels bound by all of the other truths that are not so pretty.

You see, in my adult life, I have also done some wickedly selfish things often in the same season and span of time that the wonderful things were accomplished. I have used my gifts and resources to hurt people. I have said and done things to damage my family and friend relationships. I have given up on or self-sabotaged just as many visions as I have nurtured out of my fear of failure. I have blamed so many of my seasons of downfall on my fear of failure. My fear has kept me prisoner in a dark, dim fortress.

But what I know for sure today is that it is not my fear of failure that keeps me captive. It is my fear of success. What if I succeed? What if I thrive? What if I prosper beyond my own imagination? Will I get too high-minded? Will I become conceited? Will my light shine too bright? Will my light shine too bright for those around me? Will I make anyone around me feel uncomfortable?

I come from meager beginnings and very humble people. People saw you as doing too much if you dared step outside of the box to do the un-ordinary. So I chose to excel in doing the ordinary, expected tasks of life - college, teaching job, apartment, car, etc.

Can I tell you a secret? If I lived without fear back then, I would never have attended college or began teaching. I would have run off to California or New York to sing and act for a living. So every once in a while, I wonder who or what I would have become had I lived without fear then.

My context is different now, but the lesson learned still holds true. So I am learning every day to be fearless, to let my light shine, to do the things I dream of doing, no matter what. It's a journey, but I am definitely less concerned about dimming my light to accommodate others. I just want to shine brightly to inspire others to do the same

Questions for Reflection

1. What would you do if you had no fear?

2. What makes you shy away from, dim, or hide your light?

3. What steps can you take to let your light shine brighter today?

_____

_____

_____

_____

_____

_____

_____

_____

_____

_____

_____

The Sweet Taste of Freedom

by SHAVON CARTER

For eight months, I fought to maintain a relationship with a man, when at my core I knew it wasn't meant to be. When we met, I had just released my second book "Dear Ms. Wholeness" detailing my journey of unhealthy relationships, a shotgun marriage, divorce, and healing from it all. Because I had overcome so much relationally, been in counseling for years, abstained from sex for years, and served in several ministries at church, I felt entitled to receive the desires of my heart. When my "blessing" in the form of a man didn't come, I decided to take matters into my own hands and actively pursue a male suitor. But deep down a small voice told me that I needed more time with myself. Ignoring the voice, I trudged full speed ahead into a new relationship with a man I met online, hoping that this time it would work out the way I wanted. What I didn't understand was that I couldn't manufacture someone who would align with who I was emotionally, mentally, spiritually, and professionally. Although the guy I was dating was cool, he wasn't what I truly desired. Every part of me (emotional, mental, spiritual, and physical) needed to be in agreement with what I was doing, and they weren't; which created so much inner turmoil. I tried to deny, rationalize, and justify my feelings, but they intensified to the point where eight months in, I started to feel deep anxiety that led to a knot in my chest that just wouldn't go away. My body tingled with worry and stress, my vision blurred, my spirit deflated, and my confidence lessened. At that point, I was faced with a choice: Hold onto him and lose me or let go of him and choose me. I chose the latter.

The peace I feel from letting go of that relationship reveals how important it is to live and make choices from my core. My inner self, coupled with God's spirit serves as my compass for the direction my life needs to take. It lets me know when I'm off course and lovingly shows me how to get back on track. I've tasted this freedom before, but it was always short-lived because of my underlying addiction to love. This time I chose to beef up my accountability structure by joining a love addiction recovery group so I can break free from needing a man's love more than my own love. So not only am I experiencing the freedom of letting go in service of me, I see the new beginnings of breaking a cycle that has held me captive for decades.

Sis, if you've been holding onto something or someone that's causing you constant stress or anxiety, I encourage you to fight for your freedom. Your peace is more important than anything else. Where there is peace, there is clarity, creativity, and oneness with you. Protect your peace at all costs; you're worth it.

Questions for Reflection

1. Provide your own definition of freedom.

2. What have you been fighting to hold onto that is costing you peace?

3. What steps towards freedom do you need to take today?

_____

_____

_____

_____

_____

_____

_____

_____

_____

_____

_____

_____

_____

_____

That Was Really About Me, Not Him

by DR. TRENACE RICHARDSON

I had a moment at the mall play area today. I saw myself in my son as he slowly made his way over to a little girl in the hopes that she wanted to play with him. He walked over to her and stared. He followed her for a while without speaking and seemed to be asking for permission to speak with his eyes. His words, when they finally came, were inaudible to me. But they brought tears to my eyes because his words seemed inaudible to the little girl as well. I found myself sad at my core for my son because, at that moment, someone seemed to be rejecting him; someone he wanted to spend time and space with did not feel the same. I wanted to rescue him. Turn that little girl around and yell at her. Help her understand how precious and beauti-ful my little boy is. How dare she not give him the attention and focus that he sought from her? I wanted her to know that she was missing out on his funny statements, his playful ways, his caring hugs, and his creative stories. I wanted to whisk him away from that moment assuring him that she wasn't worth it anyway, that he would later find someone who accepted him the way he was without requiring him to change first.

But I sat in my seat and allowed the tears to fall realizing that in that moment, I was sadder for myself than him. You see, soon after the disappointment of that rejection, my son simply moved on and tried to engage another little friend. It was I who could not move on, slowly becoming aware that the moment was a picture-perfect image of my own rejection issues. Whether it was from daddy issues, a former boyfriend cheating on me, or failing at something I attempted, I realized that my quest to overachieve was often a smokescreen for my real desire to be accepted, affirmed, and appreciated. And on that day at the play area, I had imposed my own neediness onto my son and wanted to rescue him the same way I wanted someone to rescue me when I was younger.

But I know that truth. As much as I hate to admit it, the truth is this is not the last day he will be disappointed. He has many more days of rejection ahead of him. It won't be because of his mommy or daddy not being there for him because my husband and I are both committed to loving that little boy with everything we have. But he is destined to be hurt, disappointed, rejected, or dismissed at some point. And if I don't allow him to experience some of that now, it is sure to devastate him later in life. So I now play the tortuous game of figuring out when to rescue him from conflict and when to let him feel the sting of disappointment so that it won't be foreign to him as he gets older. I am not writing this as a blog entry because I have the solution; quite the contrary. I am presenting it to some REAL Women as a REAL dilemma I struggle with these days.

Questions for Reflection

1. How do you deal with this issue regarding your own children or children you hold dear?

2. Perhaps you have something or someone else that is very close to your heart. How do you resist putting on boxing gloves every time someone challenges your pride and joy?

_____

_____

_____

_____

_____

_____

_____

_____

_____

_____

_____

_____

_____

_____

I'm Way Overdue

by DR. TRENACE RICHARDSON

Warning: This post includes language that may be a bit much for a woman who has struggled with getting pregnant or carrying a baby to full term. It is not my desire to be insensitive, hence this warning. I only aim to be honest and true to my own voice.

My baby should have been born ten years ago. It's amazing she's not dead inside me yet. I have no idea what has kept her alive all these years. It can't be what I was feeding her because I've been so inconsistent as a nurturer. I don't think anyone or anything could ever exist or survive on the cocktail of fear and procrastination that I have been downing. But because I made sure I drank it out of a beautifully crafted wine glass, it looked like I was giving my baby life.

The reality was I settled for just knowing I was pregnant. I became comfortable with the idea of having an idea. It felt good to have a dream conceived within me. After all, people love to see pregnant women coming, right? They save the best parking spaces for mommies-to-be. They give up their seats to let pregnant women sit down. People carry things for you when you are pregnant because they feel you are already carrying a heavy enough load inside of you. They pay you major deference when you are with child — as if you did much more than simply have sex with a man who didn't pull out.

You can dress it up as much as you want, but the truth is I didn't do anything miraculous to have a dream. Everyone has an idea at some point in their lives. No one can take credit for getting pregnant, just as no woman should shoulder the blame for not being able to get pregnant. The ability to want, to desire, to hope, or to dream is beyond us, and we have no control over the fact that we have incredible potential inside of us. Potential is nothing we work hard to conceive. It's just there. We all possess potential. The hard work comes once you decide to bring your baby full-term and give birth to what was once just a desire in your heart. And for so many years, I've been satisfied with having the potential to do the extraordinary. During this decade, I have even accomplished a few things that others might categorize as labor. But because I know the magnitude of the potential within me, I would only describe what I have done so far as a part of my pregnancy glow.

But it's not cute anymore. It's not comfortable. It even hurts to carry my potential this far past term. I have a fully grown, ten-year-old inside of me, longing to get out into the world and be. I have no more excuses. I have run out of them. This won't be pretty or easy, but it is necessary. I'm ready to push.

Questions for Reflection

1. What dream have you been carrying that it's time to birth?

2. What next step do you need to take to realize your dream?

_____

_____

_____

_____

_____

_____

_____

_____

_____

_____

_____

_____

_____

_____

_____

_____

DO NOT DISTURB
TESTING IN PROGRESS

by DR. TRENACE RICHARDSON

As the summer nears an end and parents everywhere begin the "back to school" rush with their children, I am reminded of my school days, which have probably been more than most. You see, I have been a LIFELONG student. I spent the traditional 13 years in preschool, elementary, middle, and high school. I then went on to do four years undergraduate, three years graduate, and 10 YEARS…let me repeat that…10 LONG YEARS on my doctorate in Higher Education Administration. So I am an experienced student, to say the least…okay, maybe a bit of a nerd.

You see, there were many things about school that I loved. I loved reading books, asking questions, and researching. I loved discussing theories and principles with others to come to a better understanding of what I believed. But if there was one thing I dreaded about school, it was the TESTS.

I was never a good test taker, mainly because my philosophy on tests is that they are only a snapshot of all that I have learned over a longer period. They don't accurately reflect how much I know overall. What if it's a terrible day for me emotionally or physically? What if they ask me the one set of questions I DON'T know the answer to versus the countless number I DO know? Why cause me all of that anxiety and fear? Surely there has got to be a better way than a TEST to prove whether I have learned something from what I've experienced.

But the irony is that I have also been a teacher for much of my adult life. I taught high school students for several years in Prince George's County MD, and since then I've taught count-less classes on several topics. And as a teacher, I found that there are a lot of ways to find out what a student learned from their experiences in your class. But no matter what the method, they could all still be described as a TEST. Whether written or oral, whether multiple choice or true and false, whether open-book or closed-book, whether testing by doing, reciting, problem-solving, or regurgitating the answers – they were all TESTS.

Tests could be described as "critical examinations, observa-tions, or evaluations." So whenever you have found yourself be-ing critically examined, observed, or evaluated by anyone, you were being tested. No matter what you or they called it, it was a test. A test to see if you would pass or fail; if you would show what you learned or act as if you never learned anything at all. And more often than not, the test was not really to show the teacher what you had learned because usually, that was pretty obvious by how willing you were to participate in class. The test was to really show YOU where you are in the process of learning the material. Because the truth is if you have truly learned the lesson, you will pass any test that comes your way. But until you pass the test, you must be reintroduced to the teaching until you master the material.

So tests are necessary and revelatory for us to see where we really are. And that's why we don't like tests because they show us where we really are. And usually, the tests prove that we are not as far along as we thought we were. I have often been tested in an area and discovered that I was not as strong as I thought I was. And you know I'm no longer talking about school now; I'm talking about life. Life has a way of sending tests our way that can completely knock down the self-righteous picture we have painted of ourselves. How do we handle it when life hands us relationship challenges or financial obstacles or health issues? Do we respond exactly the way we believe God would want us to or do we sometimes crack under the pressure of the test?

Well, there is a way to appropriately deal with tests so that we get the most out of them. And this may surprise you, but it's all about EXPECTATIONS. You can pass the tests that come your way if you approach them with specific expectations.

1. EXPECT TESTS TO COME

And we will never be able to avoid taking life's tests completely. We have either survived a test, going through a test right now, or a test is on the way.

2. EXPECT TESTS TO BE HARD

What I've learned is that a test is not supposed to be easy or fun. Taking a test is a serious time. It is a time of reflection; a time of trying and proving what's going on inside of you.

3. EXPECT TESTS TO MAKE YOU BETTER

Keep in mind that with any test, you will either pass it or learn from it. Either way, you are going to be better as a result. With tests, you never fail, you only pass, or you learn.

No matter what, don't fret over your tests. You will never be fully prepared for them, but if you keep these three expectations in mind, you can take a deep breath and EXPECT TO TEST WELL.

Questions for Reflection

1. How are you currently handling life's tests?

2. How can the current tests in your life help grow you?

_____

_____

_____

_____

_____

_____

_____

_____

_____

_____

_____

_____

_____

I'm Good...

by NEPHATERIA MCBRIDE

It's a chilly Thursday morning, and I'm sitting in the Cadillac dealership waiting for my car to be serviced. I have some tasks to complete while waiting, so I decided to sit in one of the workspaces the dealership provides versus sitting in front of the television. As I'm setting up my laptop and pulling books out of my bag, I quickly glance around the room and notice that I'm one of only two women sitting in the waiting area. All of the other customers waiting are men. For a brief moment, I feel a twinge of sadness because I wish that I had a man in my life to do this task for me...then I wouldn't be sitting in this Cadillac dealership either. But I quickly capture this thought and say to myself... Nah, you're good boo!

Let me explain why that last statement is so significant for me! For the first time in over 20 years, I'm not in a relationship. Some of my single ladies may be reading this and thinking...that's nothing to be happy or excited about. And some of my married ladies may be releasing deep sighs and saying "I wish!" LOL!! Whatever side of the coin you fall on, I want you to know that at this present moment, I realize that I'm good. I'm not sad that I'm not in a relationship. I'm not pressed to be in a relationship. I'm just good. For the first time in my life, I'm learning to be comfortable with me. I'm rejecting the idea that something is wrong with me because I don't have a man in my life. I'm rejecting the notion that a relationship with a man automatically equates to happiness. I'm not in a relationship. I'm happy. And I'm good!

Nope!! Before you think it, let me get you straight. I'm not angry with any man. I'm not bitter. I'm not drowning in the sea of unforgiveness. I haven't sworn off men. I'm not so hurt that I just can't fathom the thought of being in a relationship again. I'm none of those things!! At some point in the near future, I want to be in a healthy relationship. I desire to be married again and build a life with a man who is my very best friend. But, today, I'm content in the space that I'm in. I'm learning to be okay with me and operate from a core of self-love. I've written this just to say that I'm not in a relationship AND I'm good! And I'm so proud to announce that!

Questions for Reflection

1. What area of your life can you honestly say, "I'm good!"?

2. If you're not good, what can you do to be good in the midst of your situation?

_____

_____

_____

_____

_____

_____

_____

_____

_____

_____

_____

_____

_____

_____

_____

_____

_____

My Scars Are Beautiful

by NEPHATERIA MCBRIDE

If you look on the bridge of my nose, there is a small dark circle. There is a similar scar on my right forearm. Each circle is a scar caused by the chickenpox. Lol. My chickenpox scars remind me that I disobeyed my Mother and scratched those places when I wasn't supposed to! There is a faint mark on my left leg near my ankle. I was running down a hill one day and failed to notice a small pipe with a jagged edge sticking out of the ground. Needless to say, that one hurt! I ran screaming to my Grandmother's house after tumbling down the rest of the hill. A more prominent scar sits on my left knee…I skidded on rocks one day while riding my bike and skinned my knee. As painful as the wounds were at that time, the scars remind me of happy days as a little girl….days when I played hard outside and went in the house smelling like a little puppy.

Then there are the most recent scars…the three scars on my belly that mark the incision points for the surgeon who removed my ovaries and fallopian tubes in December 2016. And then there are the scars around my breasts. As I stood in the mirror this morning, my finger traced the scars that entirely outline the bottom curve of each of my breasts. These scars are a reminder of the bilateral mastectomy and immediate breast reconstructive surgery that I also endured in December 2016. The scars around my breasts also remind me of the courageous decision I made last year to reduce my risk of breast and ovarian cancer after testing positive for the BRCA2 gene mutation.

BRCA2 gene mutations account for about half of all cases of inherited breast cancer. As my Mother, Grandmother, Aunt (Grandmother's sister), Great-Grandmother, and Great-Great-Grandmother have all had breast cancer, I made the life-changing decision to get ahead of the disease and reduce my risk. And I have the scars to prove it! Although it was a life-changing, courageous decision, I was sad as I looked in the mirror this morning. You see, my nipples were removed too during the surgery. No nipples there...just another scar to mark another incision point made by the surgeon last year.

But I was only sad for a faint moment!! As I continued to look in the mirror, a sweet smile spread across my face. Yep, I'm forever marked with scars. But my scars are beautiful because they are a sign that healing has taken place! The wound has been healed!! Did you catch that?? If not, catch this! My scars are a glorious reminder of the things that I have survived! My scars tell my history. Essentially, my scars are history written all over my body. They are a reminder that I'm still here. My scars are my battle wounds...beautiful in every way. But there's more to the story...

I also have scars that can't be seen with the physical eye... scars from the loss of loved ones, disappointments, heartache and pain. The wounds that cause your heart to look like this... stitched and bandaged up. The scars that cause your eyes to fill with tears when you ponder all you have endured. I believe that these are the scars that hurt the most because we sometimes get stuck in pain from the wound that caused the injury. Therefore, I want to challenge your perception of these invisible scars. You may not think it, but these scars are beautiful too! They are a reminder that God has kept you. They are a reminder that God heals the brokenhearted and binds up their wounds (Psalm 147:3). They are a reminder that what was designed to destroy you didn't prosper. Just as your physical scars tell your history, these invisible scars tell your history too. They are your spiritual battle wounds!! Instead of being ashamed or nursing the pain that's associated with them, it's time to embrace these scars and declare that they're beautiful in every way!!

My scars helped to mold me into the woman I am today. Therefore, I am embracing every one and declaring that they are beautiful to me and beautiful to God. Will you do the same regarding your own scars? Your scars have made you who you are today. Embrace them for they are lovely. Peace and blessings to you!

Questions for Reflection

1. How can you embrace your physical and invisible scars?

2. What beautiful reminders do your scars give you?

Nothing Will Be Wasted

by NEPHATERIA MCBRIDE

I found myself in the midst of a full-blown pity party a little while ago. Not only was I having a pity party, but I also started drowning in the Sea of Regret. You know how it goes…I wish I had made better choices years ago. Things would be so different right now if I had made better decisions. I can't believe I wasted so much time in that relationship. Yep, that was me! It was pity party central!! Have you ever had one of those days?? I knew that I would continue to sink deeper into the pit of despair if I continued to rehearse those thoughts. However, I was having a tough time moving out of that place. As I continued to wallow in my self-pity, the words "nothing will be wasted" dropped into my spirit.

Those words took me to Romans 8:28. I like the New Living Translation. It says "And we know that God causes everything to work together for the good of those who love God and are called according to his purpose for them." Well, let's see. I love God. Check!! I know that I am called according to his purpose. Another check!! This shut the pity party completely down. I could not wallow in pity and rest in the promise that God will cause everything to work together for my good at the same time! I began to rejoice in the fact that NOTHING and I mean NOTHING will be wasted! God will work ALL things –the good, the bad, the ugly, the things that leave you speechless, and even the things that make me curl up in a ball and cry – together for my good.

Just in case you're not tracking with me, let me make this REAL for you!! I was touched inappropriately as a child. I became sexually active when I was in the 6th grade. I had my 1st child during my senior year in high school. I was raped when I was pregnant with my 2nd child the very next year. I aborted a child the year after that. I seriously contemplated suicide the year after that. I was so intent on proving to everyone that I could achieve the American Dream with two kids out of wedlock that I married a man I barely knew. I achieved great success in my career after college and quickly moved up the ranks in the Federal Government, but my marriage suffered in the process. I had an affair with one of my coworkers. I divorced after almost ten years of marriage. I was so ashamed of the decisions that I had made that I went on a relentless pursuit of love to try to "fix" the things that I had broken and ended up in a relationship that shattered the remaining pieces of my heart. My oldest daughter was shot and almost died three years ago. Is that REAL enough for you?? Ok, good!

Now listen!! God is taking ALL of that… every life experience, heartache, joy, and pain… and is molding it into the clay that He is working on the potter's wheel to shape me into the woman He has purposed me to be. Nothing will be wasted!

And guess what?? He can do the same for you! That means that God will work every tear you've cried, every painful experience, every heartache, and every joy together for good. So, don't despair!! Stand in confidence and know that nothing you have or are experiencing right now will be wasted. Absolutely nothing...

Questions for Reflection

1. Identify three major life experiences. How have they impacted you?

2. What treasures have come from the aforementioned experiences?

_____

_____

_____

_____

_____

_____

_____

_____

_____

_____

_____

_____

_____

_____

Walk In Your Truth

by KEAH MASON

Within nine days, I had four dates. This has never happened before! As excited as I was, I had to wonder why. Why now? For years, nothing! And then all of a sudden, I had options. Heyyyyyy!

I think this has happened for me now because my perspective has changed. Not perfect by far, but I've made some decisions. I've done some work on myself, and I'm more prepared now than I used to be. The loneliness and pain I've experienced in my life prompted me to spend time learning to accept God's unconditional love for me. Yep, God loves the single, dateless, childless thirty-five-year-old me. Once I really embraced that truth, I started loving myself too. Still such a work in progress, but little by little, I'm intentional about my self-care...providing care for myself by myself.

For a long time, I didn't understand why God was answering other prayers in my life, but wouldn't even send me a date. I realize now that I just wasn't ready, and I had my past to prove it. I've had "situationships", which were never a good thing. Yes,

I was the girl that allowed the "man in my life" to come over whenever he wanted. And you can imagine what kind of situation that led to. Not that I wanted that, but that's all it was and I accepted it because I didn't want to be completely alone. I thought a little piece of love was better than no love at all. But that WAS no love at all. I was settling big time, and I've been like that for my entire adult life. I didn't know how to change. Can you relate?

As so many doors are now opening in my life, and some others are closing, I can only say that it aligns with God's will and His timing for me. These things hadn't happened until I started embracing my truth and walking in it. That didn't mean beating myself up, but I had to acknowledge my wrong in my situations and make conscious decisions to no longer live like that. My behavior had to change. Before anyone came along at all, I only had me. I had to face myself in the mirror and vow to love the reflection I saw right now, as is. Not once a husband and children comes into the picture, but right now. I have to let go and let God's love be above all else in my life. That gives me the strength to keep believing in love, even for myself. It doesn't start with a man providing it for me…it starts with me offering it to myself and accepting it. Even when no one else invites me out, I can take myself out. My truth is that I am enough. I just want to remind you…you're enough too. Walk in your truth girl.

Questions for Reflection

1. What perspective shift do you need to make about your life today?

2. What truth can you walk in today that brings joy and peace?

_____

_____

_____

_____

_____

_____

_____

_____

_____

_____

_____

_____

_____

Believe Something Different

by KEAH MASON

In my early twenties, I started attending a women's Bible study at my church. After a few months, the leader announced that she would be leaving the church to relocate and wanted to know if there were other women interested in leading some of the women's Bible studies. I agreed, and I thought things went pretty well. Over the next few months, other women led Bible studies as well, and when the new leader of the women's ministry came on board, I wasn't asked to assist her. She was given a list of other names of potential teammates, but I wasn't on the list. I immediately assumed... I wasn't good enough.

I've had that negative feeling a lot in my life. My father was a part of my life growing up, but there were times our relationship was distant. That meant, I wasn't good enough. In middle school and high school, boys didn't ask for my number and they didn't ask me out on dates. That meant I wasn't good enough. I didn't get picked for the cheerleading squad. I wasn't voted as homecoming queen. I wasn't asked to be the leader of the young adult ministry I had helped to build. I wasn't picked to join another leadership ministry I wanted to be on. I wasn't asked to be a maid of honor or bride's maid in my friends' weddings. As always, not being picked to lead any more Bible studies must have meant…I wasn't good enough.

Now in my mid-thirties, I still don't get picked for the things that mean the most to me. For some reason, there's a deep need for me to be chosen. For someone to make me feel like they see me, and I matter to them. I'm always looking around, and I see my peers being selected and I can't help but to wonder why no one picks me. Why are all of my co-workers either married with children, or at least in a serious, committed relationship? Why are my teammates entrusted to facilitate sister circles, conferences, and workshops, but not me? Why wasn't I asked to be grade level team leader? How come I didn't get a student intern to mentor in my classroom? Why wasn't I asked to be on the curriculum writing team when I have a master's degree in curriculum and instruction?

For me, not being selected automatically translates to… I'm not good enough. Although I feel this on a regular basis, there comes a time when that lie has to come face to face with God's word. While our feelings are genuine and very valid, they are not always reflective of God's truth. Would our Heavenly Father ever say to us, "You're not good enough"? Absolutely not! Those are not His words. That's not even the essence of His character.

Sisters, I encourage you today…seek God's truth in spite of how you feel. Let His truth be bigger than your feelings. Often, our perspective can lead us to bondage. When we don't feel picked by someone, we feel rejection, denial, and lack of interest. Many times, that's not even the case, but once that seed has been planted in our minds, we take that feeling and wash ourselves in that lie every day. We make it our reality. We jump to that conclusion every time something doesn't go our way.

I challenge you today...believe something different. No matter how you feel, believe in the good and positive for yourself, about yourself.

Questions for Reflection

1. Are you struggling with feelings of not being good enough? How have those feelings impacted your life?

2. How can you shift your perspective about you and focus on the truth?

_____

_____

_____

_____

_____

_____

_____

_____

_____

_____

_____

_____

_____

Chosen One

by SHERI FAYTON

What I have come to know through my past experiences and observations in the workplace (and with my many jobs I've been afforded more opportunities to observe than I care to acknowledge), is that there are numerous occasions a job position is advertised (to follow protocol), but the hiring manager has already predetermined their desired applicant even before the hiring process starts! I know, if you're like me, you're thinking, "that's jacked up…unfair…bogus, right?" Yeah, it is, but only if you're not the "Chosen One." Just think about it…how freeing it is to be in a position that you don't have to prove, justify, rationalize, work for, or measure up in order to receive this kind of favor. The favor has less to do with the qualifications of the predetermined applicant and more about the position/ authority of the hiring manager. In other words, when a hiring manager has already preselected an applicant for a specific position, it does not matter how smart you are. How much experience you bring to the table. Who your momma and daddy is (yes, I know English Majors, it should be "are," just go with me for this example). Who you know. How many degrees you have. Or, how many letters follow your last name. If you are not the "Chosen One," you're not going to get the position…point blank, end of story. Why? Well, the boss aka "Shotcaller" has already qualified the individual he or she wants to hire to get the job done. The only thing that is needed from the preselected applicant is to be present for the position.

This analogy has helped me with the "how" in the relentless, discovery process of searching for purpose in my life. Now for a little bit of self-disclosure: I've been "that girl" who has become discouraged, frustrated, jaded, hopeless, resentful and jealous because of my vantage point always being set from the perspective of seeing other people's accomplishments/gifts vs. identifying my own specificity. Through my many disappointments (and they have been many) and seasons of feeling empty, it has taught me not to spend precious time attempting to measure myself by what I see in others, to determine my calling, my purpose, and my destiny. Their journey is not for me to covet. I've become exhausted with applying for positions that did not align with my current skillset; wishing, praying, and trying to qualify for a job assignment that was never meant for me to have.

It's so exhilarating to feel I don't have to prove myself all the time. To just be present and receive the favor my Creator has already placed on my life is a blessing itself. Now, the being present part has not been an easy feat to accomplish, nor has it been easy identifying which assignments truly belonged to me. It has required a significant amount of introspection, studying, reading, purging, healing, and making divine connections with people who believed in me and saw greatness in me even while my vision was still blurred. Once I stopped worrying about what I thought I could never be and refocused my energy on tapping into discovering who I already was, my job search became more of an exciting scavenger hunt vs. a stifling burden! The miraculous opportunities that have availed itself and favor shown in my life have invigorated my soul with a renewed sense of hope and expectation. It still, at times, makes me skeptical (in a non-paranoid-type of way) of the thought of me being the Chosen One. However, when those insidious doubts attempt to slither their way back into my thoughts, I remind myself that I have not been chosen because I'm worthy or qualified, but because of my connection to The Boss who has qualified the call and preselected me to fulfill it. Therefore, I slowly and cautiously lift my hand to gently say, "Present."

Questions for Reflection

1. In what areas of your life do you feel overlooked?

2. How would your perspective shift if you embraced that you're already chosen?

_____

_____

_____

_____

_____

_____

_____

_____

_____

_____

_____

_____

_____

_____

Image Over Truth

by SHERI FAYTON

I recently started down a journey of embracing my natural, weave-less hair. Yes, I'm a recovering weave-aholic. Now, before all of my extension-wearing sisters start rolling their eyes and judging me, let me explain. I love the versatility of going from kinky, curly big hair to silky straight, honey-blonde streaked hair in a matter of a couple of hours (well, with my former stylist, it was more like 6-8 hours, but that's another story). I absolutely adored my weave and all that it allowed me to be! Even after I started to develop a pretty severe scalp condition that caused my hair to come out around the hair line and psoriasis, I was still determined I was not going to give up my sew-ins. It was a part of how I wanted to be perceived and how people came to recognize me.

So, I began to search for wigs which would allow me to apply the medicated, prescribed shampoo and oil treatment on my hair at least once a week; a necessary process to get my scalp issue under control. I hated the wigs and disliked the similar outcome of when my stylist applied the extensions to a wig cap.

This dilemma had begun to contribute to a significant amount of angst within myself. You see, it had been years (a whole lot of years) since I wore my own hair… I had no idea what that would be or how it would look! I had admired my natural wearing Nubian Queens from afar while in the same breath proclaiming "I could never go natural!" Well at least weave-less. I had been without a relaxer for several years and swore to myself I would never put one back in my hair, which made wearing my own hair even more terrifying! Whatever laid beneath my crown of glory terrified me more than my scalp condition itself.

Reflecting back on what some may call an insignificant part of my journey, in it, were nuggets of an invaluable life-lesson. I, like many women, have become so absorbed in creating and maintaining an image at the cost of owning my truth. What I wear; how much money I make; how successful I am; what car I drive; where I live; what college I attended; where I'm employed; who my husband is; how well my children are doing; what designer clothes I wear… and the overwhelming list goes on and on. And although some of these things may have a level of relevance, I had to confess, the energy, time, and money I've poured into my image over the years contributed to furthering the distance from me owning my truth on many occasions.

I recently apologized to my daughter, Brittney, who has a kind, sensitive soul. But instead of these characteristics creating pride in her, she started to exemplify shame evinced by a burst of tears for being what she defined as being "so emotional." I realized the image I had presented to her…a mother who had to keep it together. You know that strong, black, independent, confident, superwoman that "nothing" could break down. It crushed me to know that I had done her a disservice by never sharing my truth; thus, becoming an unwilling contributor to some of her feelings of shame and being disconnected. The truth is, I'm not all strong. I have vulnerabilities. I'm not all confident; I have moments of doubt; I'm not all kind; I have moments of stubbornness & shrewdness. I'm not all patient; I have moments of abrasiveness. I'm not all knowing; there are a lot of times I don't know what the hell I'm doing. I'm not as career savvy as I wanted to once appear; there were times, in the past, I sabotaged jobs because I was so miserable and felt stuck like a caged animal because I decided to chase a dream that didn't belong to me. That is my truth. When did my image start becoming more sacred than my truth? I'm sick and tired of believing that I have to be This OR That, the truth is I'm a beautiful, hot-mess of This AND That!

Just like my infected scalp, my truth needed to be uncovered (the weave removed) in order for the healing to take root in many areas of my life. It required exposure to light and air which acted as healing agents. The process has been equally uncomfortable as scary, not knowing how my truth would look once it permeated the firewalls I had built through my imagery. However, I have come to know my truth, and my TRUTH has set me free! Free to be that fierce girl, whether wearing Milkyway, Yaky, #4 or my natural, weave-less, very-hard-to-manage-at-times hair. At this stage of the game, if had to pick between my image or my truth, I choose truth.

Questions for Reflection

1. What image have you been wearing to mask your truth?

2. What would it look like to choose truth over image? How would your life change?

_____

_____

_____

_____

_____

_____

_____

_____

_____

_____

_____

_____

_____

_____

_____

Just Breathe

by SHERI FAYTON

The air feels thick. I find myself gagging on the winds of change, tossed about in its shifting ways. It feels unnatural, suffocating, stifling, confining... hopeless. A piece of the puzzle that I'm desperately attempting to turn sideways upside down. Forcing that piece of the puzzle to fit into a position it has not been designed or molded to align with the other symmetrical shapes by which it's surrounded. Nevertheless, I keep on pushing, pressing, wishing, praying that a divine moment will come and instead of going through the grueling process of continually trying to adapt to a mold that my inner-self tells me, "you will NEVER fit," I surrender to truth, purpose, and authenticity. I allow destiny to begin the carving process. As each part of my-self: mind, body, and spirit seamlessly align perfectly in their appointed position, I take a moment to inhale and exhale...

"Ahhhhh."

For the first time, in a long time, I take in pure, unpolluted air and I think to myself... YES, I can finally breathe!

Today I begin the journey of celebrating who I was created to be and letting go of what I am not. No doubt, this will be one of the biggest challenges I have faced. However, the peace, joy, and fulfillment ascertained from this experience will be worth any cost I will have to pay. So… the journey begins. Although this is my personal story, I realize as human beings we share common experiences. And so, I invite you to connect with me as I navigate through these murky waters in hopes of coming out purged of any remnants of inauthenticity that has restricted my oxygen flow. As I begin to approach the aqua blue waters, I come up desperately sucking in the fresh, toxin-free air. And for a brief moment, glistening on top of the crystal-clear waters, I catch a glimpse of my divine, true reflection…

Questions for Reflection

1. What can you do to celebrate YOU today?

2. How would it feel to take a moment to just breathe?

_____

_____

_____

_____

_____

_____

_____

_____

_____

_____

_____

_____

_____

_____

_____

_____

_____

Why I'm Not Waiting

by BATHSHEBA SMITHEN

Writing helps me breathe, especially when I feel I'm suffocating under the weight of other people's opinions. I wrote my way to freedom. Throughout 32 years of existence I have been advised by those who have had my best interests at heart and those who are afraid; afraid of love, silence, laughter, pain, separation, joy, not measuring up, and as a result, they projected their fears onto me. I've been one of those fearful people, so I get it. There's no judgment or resentment.

In the past, I had allowed the advice of others to overrule my thoughts, leaving me no room to court my own life. Every thought was sequestered by dates with drafts of my destiny created by other people. As long as there was a jury in session to give feedback and rule on my thoughts and opinions, I sat as a witness to my own prosecution and—oftentimes— incarceration, as I awaited someone else's opinion to give me the green light about a major life decision.

But I am not there anymore. During my season of post-divorce, the death of a close friend to suicide, abandonment, mom's re-surfacing on social media (after not having seen her in 13 years), hostile-work-environment, custody battles, and family issues, so many voices flooded the gates of my mind that I almost had a nervous breakdown. I wanted to be free to use every hurt that I'd endured to help others who are hurting. However, there was one thing that stood in the way. It is the one thing that stops many of us in our tracks on the road to greatness: the need for security.

I know I'm a responsible person, but the decision I needed to make would say the contrary and would rattle my security to the core.

Going full time as an entrepreneur?!

As I shared my dream, I was presented with, again, the jury and their feedback:

"You need to get another job!"

"You have to pick up another position with a six-year-old. You will need to take care of your child."

"Save your money to hire a therapist to deal with the pressure."

"Leave your job it's causing too much stress, but look for another to ensure you have income."

"Stay, don't let them rob you of your job, and find some emotional stability."

"Go, or you won't have any peace."

AHHHHHHHH!!!!!!!!!!!!!!!!!!

People have all of the solutions but no solutions, and somehow I was the one made out to be crazy. SO... I shut everyone up, and I started writing. I wrote my heart out, literally, then I closed my eyes and did what was best for my child and me. I let God be true, and every man a liar and I claimed my purpose.

It's been one full year since I walked in faith, and now my company is making great strides. I didn't have a savings or any money when I started. I just had hope and vision.

Sound crazy?! Yes, I know...but, I decided to trust God with my entire life, a year ago, because when I started writing, I had gotten a glimpse of the "me" I couldn't see for years, and I COULD NOT turn back.

Something was and is calling me. I couldn't and still can't explain my next steps, I just have to walk them out.

Questions for Reflection

1. What external voices do you need to silence in your life?

2. What faith steps do you need to take today?

_____

_____

_____

_____

_____

_____

_____

_____

_____

_____

_____

_____

_____

_____

_____

_____

Embracing Greatness

by BATHSHEBA SMITHEN

Perhaps the light that draws us also steers us away from everyone else who finds comfort standing in the crevices of doors that were meant to be opened; hanging onto the hinges of passed by opportunities. Some of us run toward the light, while others of us, cover the light, eclipsing any chance to be more than merely shadows of what we are destined to be. Those of us who run toward the light have the responsibility of embracing our greatness to become a beacon of hope for others. To not shy away or say I told you so, but to let them see our faith shine, such that they may walk in their truth as well.

Greatness is scary. It's a thrill. It's unclear at times. But, while it may make you feel insecure, there is great security in purpose.

Have you ever known something without knowing how you know it?

That's how the call to greatness feels. It feels like a gnawing in the pit of your stomach that won't go away. Several sleepless nights full of ideas. A baby kicking you in your womb without delivery. A pesky ex who keeps calling your phone because they simply just don't get the hint.

And the call never ceases, until you pick up.

It may settle in the bed you've made in your mind with all the right comforters—quilted and fluffed in thoughts like, "This is simply not the right time." "What if I fail?" "I'm not the person for the job." But the call never leaves. It just waits…

It waits to be awakened from being anesthetized by our insecurities, and lack of effort. It waits to be acknowledged like the child who sits as you remain consumed in meaningless tasks.

There are parts of ourselves that are yet to be revealed, and I believe that deep down inside, we all hear the higher versions of ourselves calling. There is a knowing that we can't explain, but we have to get quiet. We have to quiet the voices of the naysayers and those who have the greatest influence in our lives. Sometimes our supporters may hinder us by wanting to save us from a course we must take. That rough terrain may be the very journey we need to take to be stronger witnesses of what's possible.

In 2016, I grew tired of waiting. I grew tired of other people's opinions running my life. I decided I wouldn't wait anymore. I decided I would court my destiny and embrace the journey.

The truth is…

I am powerful.

I hope you make that declaration because you are too!

Questions for Reflection

1. What does greatness look like for you?

2. What will be your next journey steps towards greatness?

About REAL WOMEN

REAL Women is a membership-based community of women interested in extraordinary growth and development. Founded by Dr. Trenace Richardson, REAL Women's mission is to create safe spaces for women to do REAL work on themselves.

REAL Women helps women CONNECT with other women in meaningful ways; grow their CONFIDENCE in who they are and what they are created to do; and become CATALYSTS of positive change in their lives and the lives of those around them.

REAL Women accomplishes this by hosting live and virtual Sister Circles, Intensives, Bootcamps, and other incredible experiences. For more information about becoming a member of this amazing movement, visit www.realwomenrock.org.

66471549R00075

Made in the USA
San Bernardino, CA
12 January 2018